KINTSUGI FAITH
RESTORING BEAUTY IN MY BROKENNESS

MENDING IMPERFECTIONS WITH GOLD & GRACE: A JOURNEY OF FAITH, RESILIENCE & RESTORATION

TYNISA HASKINS

Published by Scripted Messages, LLC Gambrills, MD
www.scriptedmessages. com

Printed in the United States

Hardcover ISBN - 979-8-9992604-0-6
Paperback ISBN - 979-8-9992604-1-3
EBook ISBN - 979-8-9992604-2-0

Library of Congress Control Number: 2025913224

Edited by Speak Fire Publishing: www.speakfirepublishing.com

Illustrations and cover art (excluding title text) by Trinity C. Haskins

All scripture quotations, unless otherwise indicated are taken from the Holy Bible, New International Version. NEW INTERNATIONAL VERSION (NIV): Scripture taken from THE HOLY BIBLE, NEW INTERNATIONAL VERSION®. Copyright©1973, 1978, 1984, 2011 by Biblica, Inc.™. Used by permission of Zondervan.

Portions of this work were refined with the assistance of ChatGPT and Microsoft Copilot, AI-powered writing tools.

This book is dedicated to my mother. She loved me deeply for as long as she was able. To her, my father and to all who battle alcoholism and substance abuse. I pray you find the freedom and peace your soul longs for.

And to the rest of us, whether you're the one struggling or loving someone through their brokenness and pain, know this: there is healing in owning our imperfections and grace in forgiving those who've wounded us.

It's never too late to be set free

It's never too late to be made whole.

ACKNOWLEDGMENTS

To my husband, Tyrone, and our children, Trinity, TJ and Tristyn; our lives have been uniquely shaped by our hardships and experiences. Yet, we've been sustained by our faith and fearlessness. Together, we've grown stronger, emerging as a new generation of resisters.

To my dear friends Renetta Hendricks and Kochitia Henderson, your prayers and encouragement have been life-giving. I sincerely appreciate your friendship and support.

To my soul sisters Jamila Hodge and Angela McCorkle; thanks for holding my hand on that Saturday when God reminded me of what He placed in my heart a few years earlier. Here's to *manifested destiny*!

To Dr. Gabor Maté (although we've never met); thank you for enlightening the world about the struggles of addiction through the lens of humanity, care, and dignity. Your written words and research convey the compassion needed to heal the sick and hurting souls of addictions. You inspire me.

May the words of this book wash over you and nourish the soil of your soul, enabling the seeds of healing to sprout up in your heart and bring forth a great harvest of hope in your life.

CONTENTS

INTRODUCTION

THE PAST DOESN'T STAY behind you, it shapes the way you see everything in front of you. The branches on my family tree connect me to three generations of alcoholism and drug abuse. Although I don't struggle with either, I feel like I'm carrying the weight of those family members on my shoulders. These strongholds have held my family captive for generations, choking joy, breaking bonds, passing down pain like an inheritance.

But I've had enough!

This cycle of pain and harm ends with me. I am not a medical professional, counselor, nor am I an expert in addiction and recovery. However, I am the daughter, granddaughter, great-granddaughter, sister, niece and cousin of people who have struggled with alcoholism and addiction. Alcoholism and addiction have been touching my life in ways I never expected since before I was born. And while society often treats it as something common, even expected; the trauma left in its wake is anything but normal.

I've felt the confusion, the heartbreak, the quiet chaos it brings. And I've learned that just because something is widespread doesn't mean it should be accepted as okay. Pain like that needs to be named, not normalized, because once you can identify the trauma, you can open the door to healing not just for yourself, but for others who are still lost in it.

This book was born out of my own journey—and it's written to encourage you to take one bold leap of faith toward healing and wholeness. For me, the pain began with my family's struggle with alcoholism and substance abuse. Yours may come from somewhere else entirely. Maybe you've already taken meaningful steps toward growth—steps that have grounded you and shaped the path you're walking now. If so, I applaud your courage and consistency.

But now, I want to challenge you to take one bigger step—the kind that moves not just your feet, but your heart. It is fueled by divine courage that transcends the seen and touches the unseen, carrying us not just forward, but upward, toward lasting change.

Throughout my life, I've taken many small steps towards understanding the mind and heart of addicted family members, but I have not fully grasped the gravity of their condition. I don't have all the answers or the right words, but my love persists.

Year after year, I kept knocking on the doors of their pain hoping to one day be let in. Not to fix it, just to listen and sit with it, so they don't feel so alone. But in the process, I began to carry their wounds as my own, absorbing their hurt until I was the one who felt isolated, overwhelmed by a pain that wasn't mine to hold.

Like me, I suspect there are others with family members and friends suffering from addiction or alcoholism, who grieve over the physical manifestation of their loved ones' pain. This book is for you. If you feel like your life's journey has left you dinged, chipped, scraped, and broken particularly because of addiction in your family, or any other past hurt, then this book is definitely for you. This text depicts the congruence between biblical restoration and the Japanese process of repairing broken objects and turning them into something just as beautiful as the original. This artistic process is known as Kintsugi. Both seek to capture the essence of healing and wholeness. Kintsugi embraces flaws and has become a metaphor for resilience, recovery and acceptance. Biblical restoration is like finding lost pieces to a puzzle (pieces we thought were lost forever) and placing them gently back where they belong, until the picture becomes whole. As you read the pages of this book, I hope you can see the possibility of experiencing true inner freedom. Perhaps, you take away something that prompts you to view life through a different lens; hopefully, with renewed expectation. So, get comfortable! There are some interesting twists and turns along this journey. But reconciliation and restoration await us!

KINTSUGI FAITH

Chapter One

CRACKS IN MY FRAME

Life isn't always fair, and faith doesn't always spare us from breaking. Though cracks deepen over time, grace holds the frame; God, my cornerstone, remains steady and sure. –Tynisa Haskins

OUR HEARTS ARE A lot like frames, meant to hold and reflect something beautiful, yet often cracked at the corners by life's weight. Some fractures are easy to spot; others stay hidden beneath layers we built for survival. Mine began in childhood, shaped by silence and the belief that strength meant staying unseen. But everything shifted when I discovered Kintsugi, not just as an art form, but a mirror into my soul. What if the places you try hardest to hide are actually where healing longs to begin? This isn't about perfection. It's about learning to see your cracks as sacred spaces where grace seeps in like gold.

For years, I learned how to live around the cracks; smiling, serving, and showing up in all the ways that made me look whole. At home, with my husband and three children, I was known. They saw the fractures and gold. But in uniform, I wore strength like armor. Nearly three decades in the military taught me how to lead, endure, and protect. Yet, very few ever saw the real me beneath the surface. The cracks were there, but I kept them hidden. Until life made it impossible to keep covering them up.

It wasn't until just three years before military retirement that I stumbled upon the courage to start sharing my story.

That turning point came with a loss that I had been bracing for, but nothing could have truly prepared me for the impact.

My mother passed away from a drug overdose during the height of COVID, so when people offered their condolences, questions naturally followed. "Was it the virus? What happened?" I was emotionally fragile and hadn't planned to say much. But their curiosity opened a door that I hadn't meant to walk through, and before I knew it, parts of my story started to slip out. It was quiet, unsure but honest. In the silence that followed, buried pain and unresolved issues from the past began to reappear. Over time, I've come to see they aren't here to haunt me; they're here to be acknowledged, to be understood. Grief, in its own way, is teaching me to listen and sit with what hurts, so that healing can finally begin. I decided to revisit my heart condition in hopes of healing my hurt.

At first, the work felt like staring at a fractured frame, disjointed pieces of my past that didn't seem to fit together. My journey has been marked by scrapes and scars, each one not just a wound, but a fragment of a larger picture I couldn't yet see. For a long time, the cracks felt random, even meaningless. But looking back now, I realize those broken edges were never lost, they were shaping the borders of a masterpiece I never knew I was creating. We all face challenges. But some of us encounter obstacles that permanently shape our trajectory. That was the case for me.

I grew up in Washington, DC, and my early years were a bit of a rollercoaster, but one thing was clear from the start: I was loved. My parents were young and unmarried when I was born. They were still trying to figure out their own lives, so raising a child together wasn't exactly easy. Their relationship never really had a label, it just kind of floated there, uncertain and undefined. After a while, my mom had to step up and figure out how to do life as a single parent. I can't imagine how tough that must've been for her. Thankfully, during those first five years, my great-aunt stepped in and gave me the stability my mom couldn't provide just yet. Her support gave my mom the chance to go to Job Corps, learn a trade, and get on her feet so she could eventually take care of me fully.

Just before I turned six, I left the steady comfort of my great-aunt's home to live full-time with my mom.

We loved each other but the bond didn't come easily, too many missed years, too much distance. She was doing her best, working hard to provide, but love in those days felt more like survival than softness. While she tried to build stability, I quietly mourned the sense of safety I had just lost.

But just as we were finding a rhythm, life threw a few more cracks my way. By the time I was 10, things had gotten harder. I didn't understand addiction, only that my questions went unanswered. My mom was worn down, doing her best to hold it all together, but the weight of it all eventually pulled her toward drugs. My dad was already lost in that world, chasing highs instead of stability. Their struggles became mine too; bouncing between homes, missed meals, and learning how to get by on my own while they were in and out of jail or lost in their own chaos.

All the moving around left me feeling unrooted, like I never really belonged anywhere. I learned how to adapt, how to fit in without getting too attached. But underneath it all, I longed for something steady. I used to wonder what it felt like to grow up in one place, with the same bedroom, the same walls, and the same familiar rhythm.

Ironically, in my search for structure and stability, I chose a career path that required constant movement. Eleven moves across different military assignments gave me plenty of connections with no real roots. Maybe that's why I became so sensitive to the unseen struggles people carry. I knew what it felt like to smile and start over while carrying the weight of uncertainty. It's easy to overlook what drives people to quietly cope, especially when their pain stays hidden beneath the surface.

Addiction often begins with a choice but over time, that choice takes on a life of its own. What starts as a way to cope, to escape, or to feel something different, eventually becomes something harder to manage, something that quietly reshapes the frame of a person's life.

So why do people turn to drugs or drink too much?

It would be easier if there were one clear answer but the truth is, each story is its own puzzle. Each reason, its own broken piece.

If you've never misused drugs or leaned too heavily on alcohol, it might be hard to understand why anyone would go down that path. It's easy to say people should know better. But no one chooses addiction, job loss, or a broken family. What they choose, often in a moment of pain or desperation is a temporary escape.

What still strikes me is how often people are caught off guard by the fallout. Even knowing the risks, the potential for destruction, they're shocked when the frame shatters. That's what happened with both of my parents. One decision led to a chain of events that altered the course of my life. And though the cracks they left behind were painful, they also revealed things I never would've seen otherwise—pieces of a story I'm still learning to piece together.

Every decision leaves a mark, some carve out pain, others carve a path to healing.

For those of us who love someone caught in addiction, the ripple effects aren't just emotional, they reach deep, touching everything. When the pursuit of the next high becomes the frame around which life is built, everything else—family, responsibility, even love can start to slip out of view.

I was one of the ones left in the margins, watching the cracks spread from choices I didn't make but still had to live with.

Without a clear mirror to show me who I was or who I could become, I started piecing together my identity from fragments of what I saw, what I felt, and what I lacked. I carried questions no child should have to carry, especially alone.

But even in the chaos, something in me held on. Some quiet part refused to break.

Growing up in that kind of instability forced me to grow up fast. I became skilled at hiding my needs, burying my emotions, and pretending I was fine when I was anything but. I learned to read the room before I even stepped inside it—always scanning, always bracing. Trust didn't come easy, and asking for help felt like weakness.

For a long time, I wore my anger and confusion like armor, not realizing how much weight I was dragging through life. The pain cut deeper with my mom, maybe because she stayed. Maybe because she tried.

And somehow, that made the cracks more complicated to carry. Remember, pain doesn't just disappear, it waits.

One of the hardest truths to face, especially as a child, is that the desire to change has to come from the person struggling; no matter how much you love them.

But when would she be ready to change?

ASK YOURSELF

- Does a broken vessel know it's broken?

- When does one realize they need to change?

I stopped hoping she'd get better and, instead, started bracing for the day she wouldn't wake up. It's a strange kind of grief; mourning someone in real time while their body remains alive. By the time I was grown, I realized I had been grieving her for years. Loving her meant letting go of her a little more each day. She was present, but not really here. It was, and still is, the slowest kind of death I've ever known—chosen, perhaps, but never truly intended.

For those suffering from addiction, the desire to change is often there. But freedom gets buried under layers of pain, shame, and survival. I didn't fully understand that as a child. I just wondered if my parents loved their addictions more than they loved me.

Sometimes, I still hear her voice echoing, "I tried."

And she did. She tried.

But peace was something she couldn't find. We were both reaching for it, just in different ways. We were trying to make sense of the broken pieces we carried. My mother never found the healing she longed for. But the cracks in my story didn't determine its end.

They became part of the path that shaped me and maybe, if you pause long enough, you'll see your own reflection in the fractures too.

Even for those of us not battling addiction, facing ourselves and truly seeing where we are inside can be one of the toughest things to do. Showing compassion is difficult when your heart has hardened to survive pain. Forgiveness is a choice; a very important one!

Choosing to forgive shows strength and freedom, not weakness. It protects your peace, guards your heart, and breaks cycles that pain would rather keep repeating.

Yes, it's hard.

But it's "heart" work, and it's worth it.

Why is it worth it?

Because everything flows from the heart, our choices, our healing, our capacity to love. As Dr. Tony Evans puts it, "just like the heart is the physical pump that keeps blood flowing through the body, our spiritual heart is the core through which God infuses life into us." If it's not working, we're not truly living, and I want to live whole and free.

Moving from hurt and brokenness to forgiveness, relief, and even reunion takes work. Real work. For everyone involved. So, if you're tempted to close the book here, I gently ask you to stay with me. Like a mirror frame worn over time, damage doesn't always show right away.

Cracks form quietly, splintering beneath the surface and shaping how we see ourselves and how we carry pain, often without even realizing it.

But here's the good news: it's never too late to tend to what's been broken.

If we're willing, God meets us there in the hidden fractures and corners and begins to fill them with strength, grace, and gold. Not to make us flawless. But to make us whole.

And maybe even strong enough to reflect a new story back to the world.

Chapter 1 Review: FRAGMENTS OF LIGHT

LOOK AT YOUR LIFE

Where in your life are you trying to "hold it all together" out of fear, rather than showing up as your whole, imperfect, beautiful self? Consider how letting go, just a little might actually invite more connection, not less. Regardless of the question, the answer awakens us to our reality and compels us to explore the condition of our hearts.

PRAY FOR CHANGE

God, my struggle and my story are important to you. Open my eyes to recognize cracks that may be hindering me from experiencing freedom. Help me release the pressure to be perfect and instead embrace the truth that I am already loved, already held, just as I am. Guard my mind from memories of past hurts and teach me to forgive. May I find courage in vulnerability and strength in surrender. Amen.

ANCHOR YOURSELF

The following verse has anchored me. Feel free to sit with it for a while or add one that's been speaking to your heart.

He has saved us and called us to a holy life, not because of anything we have done but because of his own purpose and grace (2 Timothy 1:9).

If anything in my story resonates, or if something from your own comes to mind; there's space below to reflect or share.

CHAPTER TWO

THE BREAKING

You are not too broken to be beautiful...You are
not too damaged to be used. In the unraveling,
I met something deeper; a wisdom shaped by
my wounds and a God who stayed, a constant
presence in the mess, steadfast in my healing.
−Tynisa Haskins

THE WOUNDS ON OUR soul show up in different ways, but the
truth is we're all carrying something. As we move between
who we are inside and how we show up in the world, that
damage may look different; but its weight feels familiar to
us all. Yet, in God's hands our brokenness becomes a breakthrough. Rather than hiding what's been fractured, Kintsugi
invites us to acknowledge the broken places as a healing
workspace where restoration begins.

I first heard about Kintsugi in 2021 while watching a news
segment. Something about it struck a deep chord within
me. The idea of broken things being mended with gold felt
profoundly spiritual, like a reflection of how God works in
our lives. "Rather than discarding our broken pieces, the
fragments are put back together with a glue-like tree sap
and the cracks are adorned with gold." (Tennant, 2024). God
doesn't attempt to hide the damage, instead, he highlights it
and finds beauty in our imperfections. From that moment

on, I was drawn in, spending the next few years learning more about the process and how it could reshape not just pottery, but my own understanding of healing and wholeness.

Kintsugi, in its essence, offers a way to honor our experiences, not to label them as faults.

It's in the place where hidden scars meet vulnerable healing that we find the fragile space where brokenness no longer defines us, it refines us. This is the place where we open ourselves to the beauty of being made whole. And sometimes, all it takes is a moment in front of the mirror to begin seeing things more clearly.

Mirror, mirror, what do you see?
A face that's learned to bend and be.
No one escapes the silent cries
We all hold tears behind our eyes.

Each crack we bear is uniquely our own,
A silent story, a scar we've known.
No hurt is greater, no wound too small
Brokenness comes and finds us all.

To face the mirror and truly see
Is the first step toward being free.
Naming the damage hiding there,
Invites the soul to breathe and repair.

But then what comes? What do we do
With all the cracks life's handed you?
Perhaps the healing starts with grace
Embracing brokenness, finding place.

Let's unwrap the wound, shatter lies and emerge free!

For far too long my heart has been wrapped in bandages, so many bandages that it was almost unrecognizable. A bandage doesn't heal the wound, it simply protects it. It guards what is tender, holds things in place while time and care do their quiet work. It's a covering, not a cure!

They are gentle reminders that healing needs shelter to occur. Ironically, those bandages were supposed to be temporary!

ASK YOURSELF

- Are you applying bandages frivolously?

In my case, the wounds were unseen and so deep that after every offense I added another bandage. I was not inclined to evaluate the acuteness of my wounds. Every painful moment was marked by a bandage that I wore like a proud Girl Scout. My protection became my prison; I was bound by fear and filled with resentment. I was resistant to change because that meant that I would need to consider the depth of my shattered heart.

Where do I even begin to unravel the bandages that have been holding my broken pieces in place? The heart doesn't bleed where eyes can see, which makes it hard to identify exactly where it hurts. Sometimes, words fall short of capturing the weight of the pain. And often, the fog of our circumstances makes it nearly impossible to see life beyond the hurt.

There are times in life when everything feels normal, until it doesn't. One day, you're moving through your routine, and next, something clicks...a shift...a thought...a feeling. And suddenly, you're seeing things you've somehow missed all along. Like the fog has been lifted and now the air is finally clear. That's how it started for me. Not with some dramatic moment of emotional collapse, but with the slow unveiling of the open cracks in my heart. The kind of breaking that happens quietly over time, beneath the surface.

Bruising looks different for everyone; some people wear their wounds on the surface. Those who do are quick to take offense and hyper-aware of tone or phrasing. That is because they've learned to expect harm, even in harmless moments. While for others, bruising manifests in more subtle ways, like withdrawal, defensiveness, perfectionism, or pushing people away before they can get too close. Whether it's a bruised ego, shattered confidence, or the sting of betrayal, those bruises serve as painful reminders of hurt.

The pain is the same; it just finds different ways to speak.

Sadly, my pain has showed up in all of these ways, especially offense.

And I know that because I can come off like I'm too sensitive, or like I take things the wrong way, overreacting to stuff that shouldn't be a big deal. I've heard it before, "Don't be so dramatic," "You're reading too much into it," or "I didn't mean it like that." And maybe from the outside, it does look that way. But here's the thing I wish more people understood: I'm not just reacting to what's in front of me. I'm reacting to everything that came before it.

See, I've been through some things. I don't say that for pity. I say it because it's the truth. I've learned (the hard way) what it feels like to be talked down to, ignored, shamed, left out, lied to. I've had people I trusted use their words like weapons or leave me questioning my worth, even when they weren't really saying much at all.

So, when something feels even a little like that, when someone raises their voice, rolls their eyes, or makes a joke that cuts too close, I feel it all over again. My body goes tight. My chest locks up. My mind starts racing: What did I do wrong? Am I not good enough? Are they mad at me? Should I apologize?

ASK YOURSELF

- Have you ever responded this way? Have you been wounded by words?

It's not that I want to be this way. It's that I've spent years walking on emotional eggshells, and my brain is trained to spot danger even when it's not really there.

It's exhausting.

I wish I could just let things roll off. I wish I didn't second-guess every conversation for hidden meanings. But trauma doesn't go away just because you tell it to. It lingers. It rewires you. And some days, it feels like I'm still fighting ghosts other people can't see. So no, I'm not "just offended." I'm hurt. I'm triggered. Pieces of my heart are shattered in new places. I'm trying to protect myself the only way I know how. And I'm working on it, but healing takes time. Understanding helps more than you know.

Sometimes, I just need someone to ask, "Hey, are you okay?" instead of, "Why are you like this?" Behind the reaction is a story. One I didn't choose, but one I'm still trying to rewrite.

My childhood had one major question, unanswered, though repeatedly asked.

What did *I* need at that moment?

Most of the time, I needed acknowledgment of my struggle.

And what about my own trauma? I question whether there was room for my wounds to breathe back then. Was there ever a moment for someone to notice the quiet ache of a child growing up in the shadow of addiction? My tender heart wondered:

I'm coming undone! Lord, why is the pressure so forceful? The walls on all sides seem to be closing in. I'm standing in the middle of everywhere but going nowhere, only looking up in anticipation of deliverance. Reframe the pictures in my mind and allow me to see a path forward through my pain. If you must, then unravel me so that I can be made whole.

My perspective was once shaped by hurt and dulled by disappointment. Though my wounds were invisible, they formed emotional scabs and callouses meant to numb the pain. And yet, certain triggers would tear them open again, flooding me with sadness or agitation I couldn't explain. What seemed trivial often wasn't; it was the past resurfacing in a whisper, reignited by the smallest spark. Sometimes we face things too heavy to carry or even comprehend, the weight overwhelms us and we crack. Searching for answers can feel challenging and uncertain but I had to be willing to remove those bandages.

While my pain was never acknowledged because the focus was always on my mother's needs. God sent me a sweet soul to stand beside me, the day my path crossed with Tyrone, my husband. Fate had other plans when it brought two twelve-year-old kids together, neither of us knowing we'd found our forever in each other that day. From playing outside in the neighborhood to navigating life's storms together, my husband has been my anchor through every season.

Many of us have been shattered in one way or another. While we have figured out ways to maneuver around our brokenness; we could benefit from the gentleness of a much-needed repair.

The depth of repair often depends on the wound and the scar it leaves behind. Some wounds are fresh, tender to the touch, while others have aged, triggering guarded reactions before they're even felt. But whether recent or old, pain marks us, and healing is still needed. Undoubtedly, how you identify with your hurt and pain will influence how you embrace your decision to be restored. These marks—our scars become more than reminders; they become bridges. They allow us to relate to others in their brokenness, offering hope through our testimony. We become image bearers that cannot be duplicated because of the uniqueness of our cracks. In this way, we reflect God's handiwork; cracked, yes, but intentionally restored. Our fractures don't disqualify us; they distinguish us.

ASK YOURSELF

This is a critical point of consideration.
- Will you choose the distress of the past or the redemption of the present?

No one had to tell me that something inside of me wasn't quite right, I could feel it and I didn't want to feel that way any longer. I could've continued with status quo, but I also wondered what I would miss out on if wandered along without being my "whole self." So, I decided it was time to do something different.

Kintsugi's slow and deliberate process of mending each piece with gold is much like overcoming life's challenges; it requires patience, resilience, and careful refinement to reach a state of strength and stability. The only person who knows how long this process takes is you because it's your heart, but the exciting part is...once you undergo repair, you can move forward with healing.

God's light is hope and direction towards a path of peace. I hope He shines His light through the darkness, gently exposing the "stuff" that causes us to bruise and break in places others can't see. Not to shame us, but to heal us. May His light reveal the hidden cracks we've learned to cover, so that instead of hiding them, we can offer them back to the One who restores.

Because in His hands, even the most fractured pieces become places where grace is poured and beauty begins again.

Chapter 2 Review: FRAGMENTS OF LIGHT

<u>**LOOK AT YOUR LIFE**</u>

There comes a point when you realize that the way you've been living, numbing, hiding, or pushing through can't carry you any further. I was there. I recognized the cracks forming from the weight of what I tried to ignore. Do you want to change, but don't have all the answers? Even in fear and uncertainty, choose to face the fractures, believing that growth is possible in the middle of the mess.

<u>**PRAY FOR CHANGE**</u>

God, I surrender my scattered pieces into Your hands. You are the Potter, and I trust that even the most broken parts of my story are not beyond Your repair. Use the pieces I've tried to hide as part of the story You're still writing. I trust that You can bring beauty from my brokenness and strength from my surrender. Amen.

<u>**ANCHOR YOURSELF**</u>

The following verse has anchored me. Feel free to sit with it for a while or add one that's been speaking to your heart.

> He heals the brokenhearted and binds up their wounds (Psalm 147:3).

If anything in my story resonates, or if something from your own comes to mind; there's space on the following page to reflect or share.

PICKING UP THE PIECES OF MY BROKEN LIFE

Being broken is not being ruined but being made ready. Each crack is a map; each scar, a seam of gold. What was once shattered, now shines. This is not perfection restored, but beauty reimagined. –Tynisa Haskins

So, HOW IS A broken heart made whole?

The truth is, matters of the heart can't be measured or mapped out like a plan. They're tender, deeply personal, and often shaped by things we can't quite explain; losses, disappointments, betrayals that leave quiet cracks beneath the surface. It can be challenging to confront a crack that you can't see; especially like the ones hidden inside of us. And sometimes, when life shatters us, we wonder if it's even worth trying to gather the pieces. Is wholeness still possible when we feel scattered and worn thin?

Yes. It is possible.

Not in the way we imagined, and not by pretending the pain never happened. This isn't about blame, it's about bravery. The kind of courage it takes to stop running, turn around, and begin picking up the pieces of your life with intention, trusting that healing isn't just possible, it's already reaching for you.

Have you ever accidentally shattered a glass bottle or porcelain plate? If so, you probably tried to account for every last piece—right? It's not easy.

The smallest shards scatter in places you wouldn't expect. And if that's true for something as simple as glass, how much more difficult is it to gather the broken pieces of a wounded heart?

When I've swept up glass with a dustpan, I've noticed I don't just collect the fragments, I also pick up dust, dirt, and other things that don't belong. That's how healing can feel, too. It's not just about finding what was broken but also sifting through what doesn't serve you anymore. Some things, old mindsets, false narratives, lingering guilt have to be separated and let go. Because if the residue remains, the gold can't bond. Purging and sifting aren't easy, but they're essential. They clear the space for true repair, so what's being restored isn't just put back together; it's made stronger, cleaner, and more whole than before.

Satan sows' brokenness through lies, convincing us that our actions carry no weight and have no consequences. But every time we follow that deception, it pulls us further from the closeness we crave with God and others. But even in the fallout of those choices, God doesn't turn away. He begins the careful work of repair and removes what hinders our healing, so He can draw us closer to Himself and the life He's always intended for us.

These words echoed in my heart when I began to gather my pieces:

> *As I look into this mirror,*
> *I contemplate what I can see clearer,*

If I reshape what's seen on the outside,
Will that quiet the ache I carry inside?

"I'm different now," I boldly claim
My broken pieces hold no shame.
No more time for shallow cures
I seek the kind of healing that endures.

Wait. What if I change the crowd I keep?
Will wisdom come, or will the silence cut deep?
Hurry now. I need this pain to cease
Is peace of mind real, or is the cost far too steep?

I'm ready to shift, to leave the past
To make a choice that holds and lasts.
No more returns to old attacks
This time, my heart won't turn back.

I want, no, I need a brand-new start.
No more tiptoes
This yielding feels right for my aching heart.

Often, pottery is considered useless once it's broken; hence, our typical feelings of unimportance and forgottenness. Yet, one of the best lessons I learned, is that even scraps have value and can still serve a purpose.

I can certainly attest to this.

I was a "whole hot mess" with various unassuming cracks and damage that enabled me to fool many and function like normal, until I started forgiving myself and others. Forgiveness can feel like forward motion. Forgetting the pain; that's where I stumble.

The frames of our heart hold memories from moments in time that don't just fade; they linger in the ordinary. Everyday moments can become landmines. A news segment, a familiar street, or a scent become explosives. Reminders like those and other images (such as watching someone sell drugs to your relatives) embed themselves in your spirit. Those are the memories that influence how you trust, how you love, how you cope. It's hard to stay present when the past keeps interrupting, isn't it?

How about you?

For me, the echo of my parents' addiction left cracks I didn't know how to name. My withdrawal reflex still sits close to the surface, like pulling your hand away from a hot stove. It's fast, instinctive, protective. The body remembers the heat, the burn, the lingering ache and whispers, *never again.*

Depending on the season, we might respond by running, numbing, or shutting down altogether. But none of those reactions lead us toward healing. They protect us for a time, yes, but they also keep us from fully living.

At some point, the pieces have to be examined, not just avoided. That's where the real work of restoration begins. Before the gold can fill the cracks, the breaking must be lived through, and that process can be messy, raw, and real.

My breaking happened over eleven military moves, career changes, and life's ups and downs. I've been guilty of reliving a hurtful experience and acting on those battle-worn emotions. Learning to respond from a healed place instead of a wounded one is an ongoing process. It is constant, working on the delicate balance as both wife and mother. Yet, Tyrone and I remained inseparable. His patient love and unwavering faith helping to heal my fragile heart time and time again. As a wife, I carry the weight of my past like an invisible rucksack filled with lessons, wounds, and survival instincts I still struggle to put down. I love fiercely, but the scars from years of neglected pain make trust feel like a delicate balancing act. Communication is a minefield, where words can feel too sharp or silence too loud.

I want to rely on my husband completely, to let his love soften the edges of my guarded heart, but vulnerability is a skill I'm still learning even after twenty-seven years of marriage. His patience is my refuge, his kindness is an anchor when old fears threaten to pull me under, and his sense of humor keeps my heart smiling.

In the quietest moments, I grapple with an unspoken fear that I might unknowingly repeat the same mistakes my mother made, that somehow, I could fall into the patterns I worked so hard to escape. As a mother, I wrestle with the tension between wanting my children to be fearless and knowing the world isn't always kind to the trusting. I watch them step into their own journeys, making choices that shape the paths ahead. Meanwhile, I pray they hold onto their light in a world that can sometimes feel shadowed by deception. I want them to build real, lasting connections, but the uncertainty of who is truly worthy of their trust is a concern I carry.

Have I equipped them with enough wisdom? Enough discernment? Have I made them strong without making them guarded? The past has taught me caution, but my greatest hope is that my children walk forward with open hearts that are protected but never closed.

And then there's the ache I don't always have the words for.

It comes from the part of me that longs for a maternal presence in my own life, the guidance I never had.

And though I've carved out my own path, that missing piece still lingers, quietly but constantly tugging on my heart. I carry that with me every day.

But as I said, my husband has been a mirror that reflects not my flaws, but my strength through them. If we don't consciously confront and heal our pain, we will inevitably, often unconsciously, pass it on to others, becoming carriers of the very wounds we longed to escape.

Looking back, I can see God's fingerprints all over my story. It's hard to imagine beauty when all you feel is broken. But healing doesn't always begin with answers; it often starts with the courage to believe that something new can emerge from what feels ruined. Kintsugi teaches us that beauty can rise from the very place of breakage, often through pressure, heat, and time. Like gold refined by fire, our hearts are shaped in the struggle, not in spite of it.

But not all fire refines, some fire consumes. Don't you agree?

Sometimes, the flames that surround us weren't sent to purify, but were sparked by our own unresolved pain. Have you ever been in a place where you realized that a trail of fires was following you, only to later learn that you were the match lighting those flames? James 1:20, says "human anger does not produce the righteousness that God desires"; my heart desires to be a light not a lighter. So instead of despising the breaking, lean into it; because it's often in the sifting through the ashes and gathering the scattered pieces that we begin to see what beauty God can form in us, not just after the fire, but because of it.

ASK YOURSELF

- What might it look like to invite God into those broken places? *(Reflect on areas of pain, failure, or disappointment that you may have felt ashamed of. How might God's grace work through those very places to bring healing, beauty, and testimony?)*

- Does the path you're on challenge you to heal and grow?

I can tell you, the longer you wait, the harder it gets to believe you're still worth saving. But even in that hidden place, God sees. He draws near to the brokenhearted, offering mercy—not judgment and the gentle reminder that no one is beyond His reach or redemption. And when I take a step back and trace the moments of my story, I realize just how gently and faithfully God has been present all along.

The truth is: **the time for transformation is *always* now.**

If you feel like you're too far gone, too shattered to be put back together, I dare you to stop waiting for the perfect moment. Stop hoping change will just happen. Chase it. Fight for it like your life depends on it, because it does. Healing does not come to those who simply hope; it comes to those who create an opportunity for God to respond to your offering of broken pieces.

You may not have a clear picture of wholeness right now, and that's okay. What matters is that you've taken the time to gather the scattered pieces of your heart so that you can become living Kintsugi masterpiece, made new by the Master craftsman.

Chapter 3 Review: FRAGMENTS OF LIGHT

LOOK AT YOUR LIFE

Think about the broken pieces in your life right now. Deep within each of us, echoes a quiet, distress signal. It is an unspoken cry for help, yearning to be heard beneath the noise of our daily disguises.

To truly live with depth and purpose, we must dare to turn inward and explore that signal, following its thread to uncover what it's trying to teach us about who we are and what we need. What might it mean to trust Him not only to restore you, but to shape you into something new with each golden seam?

PRAY FOR CHANGE
Lord, I come to You with a heart that feels fractured, worn by disappointment and things I can't always name. For a long time, I've tried to hold it all together, to press on without truly facing what's been hurting inside me. I'm tired of pretending I'm not hurting; today, I choose honesty. I admit I'm broken. Help me believe that healing is possible, even when it feels slow or uncertain. I'm ready to move forward with You. Amen.

ANCHOR YOURSELF
The following verses have anchored me. Feel free to sit with it for a while or add one that's been speaking to your heart.

> God, pick up the pieces of my life. Put me back together again. I give you my praise (Jeremiah 17:14).

> God, your God, will restore everything you lost; he'll have compassion on you; he'll come back and pick up the pieces from all the places where you were scattered (Deuteronomy 30:3-13).

If anything in my story resonates, or if something from your own comes to mind; there's space to reflect or share.

EXAMINING MY HEART

Pain tried to define me, but it did not finish me.
Each moment I thought I was alone; grace was
quietly working. I wasn't saved in a single instant;
I was restored slowly and steadily, by love that
refused to let me go. –Tynisa Haskins

IF I COULD HAVE fixed myself, I would've done it long ago.
It would've spared me so much stress and heartache (yeah,
right!). The hardest thing is facing your own reflection and
asking, "How did I get here?" Maybe it was something done
to you. Maybe it was a choice you made. But either way,
something sacred happens when we stop avoiding the mirror and begin examining the frames of our heart; the beliefs,
patterns, and pain we've used to hold ourselves together.

The truth is, your heart still holds the wisdom, and your
hands still carry the pieces that can lead to your healing.
Restoration begins right there, in that honest pause, when
we stop hiding the damage and start honoring the story
behind each fractured frame. The process may be slow, but
the heart can be made whole again, piece by piece, and with
purpose.

While transformation begins with a personal decision,
it doesn't happen in isolation; it unfolds in communion, in

community, and in the presence of the One who created us, the Master Potter. When we think of Kintsugi, where broken pottery is mended with gold, we have to ask: if we are the broken pieces, who is restoring us?

In theory, we are active participants in our healing. Real transformation only begins when we choose to examine ourselves to really see and understand the fractures within, consider what we share openly, what we keep tucked away, and what we've buried so deep we barely recognize it ourselves.

JOHARI'S WINDOW

I didn't have language for that kind of examination and introspection until thirteen years into my military service, a world defined by structure, duty, and discipline, when I was introduced to a tool called Johari's Window a decade before I learned about Kintsugi. The Johari Window is a psychological model used to enhance self-awareness and improve interpersonal communication.

At the time, I thought Johari's Window was just another leadership tool. I thought of it as one more framework to help manage teams or build cohesion. But as I sat with it, something deeper clicked. Slowly, it became more than a concept. It became a mirror of my soul, a puzzle to explore my own heart, piece by piece.

Together, Johari's Window and Kintsugi gave me language for what I had long felt but couldn't express; how brokenness and self-awareness can coexist. Offering practical insight into what God was already revealing spiritually. Johari's Window helped me see the truth of who I am, while Kintsugi reminded me that even the broken pieces, when surrendered to God, can become part of something beautiful and redemptive.

As I studied Johari's windows, it slowly came into focus. I didn't recognize all the pieces at first.

They were framed in mystery, with fragments of truth, long-held secrets, parts of myself I rarely show to anyone.

Each one of those fragmented windows shows a different part of me. The first window is wide open, and sunlight pours through. This is the Open Area; what I know about myself, and others know too. Maybe I'm talkative, thoughtful, or creative. It's the part of me that I'm not afraid to share. It's comfortable here. Yet, comfort doesn't compel you to change.

Still, there were parts of me I couldn't see clearly, behaviors and beliefs I thought were strength, but were really self-preservation masked as resilience. What seemed harmless became harmful because my hard work was rooted in insecurity, it caused me to remain blind to the root of my problems.

My blind spot in Johari's Window holds truths others can see in me that I'm often blind to myself. I didn't know how much I was hiding behind perfectionism or how deeply my need to 'keep it all together' was rooted in fear of being exposed. What I thought was composure was sometimes read as detachment. And what I saw as ambition was, at times, avoidance.

Perfectionism can feel like control, but it often comes from a place of deep insecurity. I was trying so hard not to fall apart that I didn't realize I was building walls instead of bridges. But just beyond those bridges lies another part of me less visible, harder to name the habits and beliefs I didn't always recognize as coping mechanisms, yet they quietly shaped my story.

This is where the Hidden Area begins, the parts of myself I know but keep tucked away from others. It's the pain I mask with a smile, the doubts I silence with busyness, the insecurities I hide behind achievement. This window of the heart has curtains. You know what's behind them, but you choose not to open them to others. These hidden pieces are often shaped by fear, fear of judgment, rejection, or vulnerability. But they matter, because even in silence, they speak.

I can hear them say:

Oh please, mirror, stop showing me
Reflections of past iniquity.
I look at now, but all I see
Is how the past still shadows me.

Please cast a shadow on what's behind,
So, I don't dwell or rewind time.
This story I'm writing, still unfolding fast,
Deserves a better end than its past.

The mistakes of one generation
Should not define the next;
New perspective, different paths
Bring meaning to my life's text.

If the blood of my ancestors still stains the air,
And lingers heavy in hearts that care,
This wound defies what words can say.
Oh healing, come. Don't delay.

What have you kept hidden in order to survive, to be accepted, or to feel in control?

Though I have never used drugs like my parents, I developed addictive behaviors by using work to escape my reality. I've been working since I was fourteen, driven by the belief that if I worked hard enough, I could shape the outcome (at least a little). I became deeply performance-oriented, clinging to the comfort of control in a world that often felt unpredictable.

And self-examination revealed why performance mattered so much. My extended family was my greatest source of pain and persecution. I've faced silent judgments, especially when my choices didn't match their expectations of how I should've cared for my mother. It felt like they saw the younger version of me, not the woman I've become. I longed to be seen, not just for where I came from, but for who I am now.

When that didn't happen, I questioned my worth and my voice. But God, in His loving way, defended me, revealing what they couldn't see and showing me what He'd always seen: that my growth wasn't performative, it was real. I didn't need to prove myself to be whole.

If we're waiting for some perfect, pivotal moment to change, when will it ever come? God, our Master Potter, is already ready, patiently waiting for us to say yes, so He can begin making all things new.

The invitation to pause, reflect and give God space to tend to what's broken in my heart, mind and hands didn't feel like control, it felt like surrender. And that was hard for me. My life felt fragile, like one wrong move might scatter everything again. The journey of restoration is rarely smooth. I started to see that healing isn't a straight line, and it's definitely not about covering up the cracks. It's about choosing, every day, what I let fill them.

ASK YOURSELF

Through an honest, courageous examination of your own heart, you can learn your heart's status. Pause for a moment to consider these questions about your own heart.

- Are you open to the kind of examination that leads to restoration?

- Do you have someone in your life whom you trust and give permission to share what they see in you that you cannot see?

Their shared insight may serve as a mirror revealing parts of you that have been hidden, even from yourself.

My effort to appear strong meant I rarely showed vulnerability, which made it harder for others to connect with me authentically. I held people at arm's length without meaning to, not realizing that my self-protection might be interpreted as indifference. Letting people in meant opening the door to parts of my life I wasn't ready to reveal.

Yet, this is what allowed me to see the invisible barriers I had fortified around my heart.

What began as invisible barriers quietly evolved into fortified walls built on lies that convinced me I was protecting myself from being hurt again. But I began to recognize the subtle ways God was reaching out to me, even when I felt emotionally limited.

He's reaching out for you, too.

There's more to me than even I can fully grasp and it shows up in Johari's most mysterious window: the Unknown Area.

It's dark, not because it's scary, but because it's unexplored. You don't know what's there, and neither does anyone else. It could be untapped talents, hidden potential, or parts of you yet to awaken. What we don't recognize or realize about our emotions, annoyances and pain cannot be healed and transformed for purpose. I've come to believe that transformation doesn't just reveal who you are, it also uncovers who you've yet to become.

In the quiet whisper of God's presence when you've run out of words to pray. His expression of love gently dismantles the lies, brick by brick, replacing them with truth that heals and grace that covers. We begin to see that safety was never meant to be found behind walls, but in the One who knows our pain and still chooses to draw near. Embracing that truth has shifted my perspective, giving me permission to release survival mode and make space for the kind of healing that leads to real renewal.

Healing asked something different of me; it asked me to let go to see the windows up close. The irony of this examination, is that, it's the last opportunity in the Kintsugi process to see yourself in your broken state before the gold glue is applied, to remember your struggle and your strength.

Moving forward means embracing the lessons learned and the strength gained from every stumble. That is what this book is about.

My restoration didn't come all at once, it came in fragments, like slivers of light breaking through the dark, just enough to show me the next step. Your journey can't take place overnight because healing doesn't follow a schedule, and transformation isn't rushed. You simply summon a tiny amount of courage the size of a mustard seed; enough to commit to restoration.

Chapter 4 Review: FRAGMENTS OF LIGHT

LOOK AT YOUR LIFE

If your instinct has been to reject anything or anyone that might stir painful memories, let's choose a new path, one where we invite God to reveal His heart toward us in a way that reshapes our understanding of true love and grace. Endeavor to summon a tiny amount of courage, the size of a mustard seed, to commit to restoration. Don't worry about how big your faith is; focus on how big the object of your faith is. Not a lot is required to genuinely believe that change for you is possible and today is that day.

PRAY FOR CHANGE

Lord, my thoughts are consumed with anxiety over my current condition. You see the cracks I've hidden and the pain I've buried deep. I surrender what I've tried to hold together on my own. Take these broken pieces and do what only You can mend me with your mercy, shape me with your grace, and let your glory fill the places that once felt empty. I place you at the center of my mind and my concerns in your hand. Help me to trust that I am still being made whole, one quiet moment at a time. Amen.

ANCHOR YOURSELF

The following verses have anchored me. Feel free to sit with them for a while or add one that's been speaking to your heart.

Examine yourselves, to see whether you are in the faith; test yourselves (2 Corinthians 13:5).

Search me, Oh God and know my heart; test me and know my anxious thoughts (Psalm 139:23-24).

If anything in my story resonates, or if something from your own comes to mind; there's space on the facing page to reflect or share.

LACQUERED LOVE

I wonder what the Artisan whispers to the canvas
before breathing life into a masterpiece. Do you
trust me? Close your eyes. –Tynisa Haskins

LIFE HAS A WAY of breaking us open in silent, sometimes invisible ways until, one day, a single fracture feels like it shatters everything. In that moment we're faced with a critical
choice: to remain in a state of disrepair, numbing ourselves
to the pain, or to surrender to the slow, intentional process
of restoration. God's love meets us in our brokenness and
His divine restoration marks our scars with healing.

This is where the resin in Kintsugi is introduced.

Traditional Japanese Kintsugi process uses urushi lacquer (similar to resin) to repair broken pottery. It serves as
a powerful metaphor for a renewed bond; illustrating the
compassionate focus and attentive care given by the repairer. God is our restorer and repairer, our life experiences
and imperfections served as fuel for growth in this moment
through His grace.

Our hearts are delicate vessels, handcrafted, unique, and
once whole. Now God, the Master Artisan, is not rushing
to replace our broken heart, but patiently restoring it. He
doesn't cover the damage. He highlights it like the gold in

Kintsugi pottery, filling every fracture with grace, making the brokenness beautiful.

This isn't surface work. It's deep, soul-level restoration. It is not a patch job, but a transformation.

Kintsugi honors that transformation by demonstrating the value of each broken piece with personalized attention, care, and handling. The goal of the repair is to bind the breaks of your heart (and rebuild it for purpose). "The resin (glue) represents the path that we walked to regain our sense of wholeness" (Altman A, 2018). This artistic visual allows us to grasp the essence of healing through sealing the seams of brokenness.

I wonder how the heart truly heals? The complexity of what we cannot see is what causes us to love so unconditionally and hurt so deeply. Sometimes the unseen threads of our soul:

- wounds from the past

- unspoken pain, and

- inherited patterns

weave themselves into our present, showing up as broken relationships and chains we didn't realize we were still carrying. But when we invite God into the tangled web, He doesn't just cut us loose, He gently unties what's bound and draws us back into community with Himself, where true healing begins.

Johari's model served as a guide to my development through self-reflection and personal action. It offered me an axis of analysis to deeply examine my heart and this part of the Kintsugi process does the same.

It invites us to take a closer look at every jagged edge, making sure each crack is carefully cleaned and sometimes filed to ensure a good fit. Every piece matters. Each one holds a unique place in the story of your restoration. Each season, experience and hardship added a new crack to my heart. Some cut deeper than others, depending on the weight they carried, but each left its mark.

How can the heart be one of the strongest muscles in the body, yet still be so fragile?

The mending is not just as a physical repair, but a transformation of our very mindset and being. The lacquered application doesn't return the object to its original form. Instead, it redefines it. In the same way, healing invites us to adjust how we see our pain, not as the end of our story, but as the beginning of a new one.

It's not just about being put back together, it's about becoming something altogether different, and beautifully whole.

Sometimes, the hardest moments come just before the breakthrough. When you're watching something painful unfold, that breaking is where God begins His work of transformation. When you've been wounded and separated, sometimes, connection feels like a risk rather than refuge.

Restored connection is not only vital to healing, it *is* the healing. As Altman writes, "Connection is the name of the game, not perfection. Healing happens in connection, not perfection." It's a truth I'm still learning, that even when my reflex says "retreat," my healing may depend on reaching back toward others, gently and intentionally. As I lean into my faith for strength, the chaos that was in my closest relationships, no longer unravels me, it reveals what God's redemptive power can do.

There is power in connection first to God, and then to the community that surrounds us. These bonds have the capacity to heal what has long been broken, to interrupt those patterns passed down like inheritances. In my own story, the weight of generational trauma marked by alcoholism, addiction, and silence became a kind of connective tissue.

It bound lives together through pain more than through love. But like the art of Kintsugi, God began to mend those fractured places, not by hiding the breaks, but by filling them with grace, truth, and connection. What once held us together in brokenness now has the potential to bind us in healing.

My connection to God not only opened the door to re-shape my story, but it also revealed that the story was never mine alone. Through faith, I've come to see that what felt like fragments were never wasted; they were pieces waiting for divine placement. In Him, my flaws became fuel to light my lamp. What I once saw as weakness, He is using as testimony.

He holds the key to my distinct, imperfect beauty, loving me in the wonders shaped through trial, loss, and grace. In His presence, I've discovered that trust isn't built on certainty, but surrender. And though my ability to trust others is still tender, God continues to send people in my path to restore my belief that He can bless every shattered part.

I spent twenty-five years trying to forget about those shattered pieces and challenges I faced with my parents' addiction. As I try to forget the pain, I risk forgetting all the important moments that shaped me. Even my mistakes play a role in what God's doing with my life. I'm in awe of my significant insignificance, and that beautiful truth keeps me humbled and helps me move forward one step at a time. And yet, even in my smallness, I'm reminded that I still have a place in something far greater—in the heart of a God who sees me, holds my story, and invites me into divine connection and purpose.

Being restored by God didn't just make me whole, it made me truly useful in ways I never thought possible. Each choice to forgive, each moment of honesty, each quiet prayer became part of the gold. Deliberate lines of restoration that didn't erase the pain, but made something new from it. And the more I leaned into that process, I realized: the pieces didn't need to go back exactly as they were because they were being reshaped, repurposed, made even more beautiful not in spite of the breaks, but because of them. Each piece, now aligned not perfectly, but purposefully.

ASK YOURSELF

- As you're being reshaped, if you could, would you do something different with your life?

- Can you recognize any "lacquer" in your journey, moments where healing, growth, or deeper connection with God has begun to fill in the broken places? *(Take time to name the evidence of restoration. What small victories, shifts in mindset, or moments of grace remind you that healing is happening, even if slowly?)*

Even after choosing restoration, I found that certain areas of healing stalled, often because of my own complacency. Mentally, I was ready to move forward, but emotionally, I hadn't taken the necessary steps. I did all the outward things associated with letting go of the drama, but healing requires more than performance. It demands presence. Standing firm in your faith or your growth doesn't mean standing still.

But I wasn't moving because I was avoiding certain people, certain memories, certain truths. I closed off those wounded places, sealing them with silence rather than gold. I tried to win my emotional battle my way and not God's way and my healing was delayed by my hostile approach. Romans 12:19 spurred me with these words, "Do not take revenge, my dear friends, but leave room for God's wrath, for it is written: "It is mine to avenge; I will repay," says the Lord." I needed to align my emotions with the truth of His love and that response took time. But true Kintsugi repair doesn't rush the process or skip over the brokenness. It honors each crack with intention as the artisan reconnects those valuable pieces.

Just as no two vessels break the same way, our healing journeys are unique. Yours may not mirror mine, so don't try to make your broken pieces fit into someone else's frame. It won't work because you may lose pieces of yourself that make up your testimony. Allow yourself to be refined with resin so you can be restored!

I cherish every single crack that's been meticulously mended, because each one tells a story of triumph. Though still visible, they no longer speak of weakness; they shine with evidence of grace, growth, and resilience. This is the beauty of becoming whole: not in returning to what once was, but in altering what remains with the lacquer of God's healing and love. When I pause to breathe and take it all in, my cup truly overflows with gratitude and joy. And you know what?

I am a living, lacquered Kintsugi masterpiece, made new by the Master craftsman.

And you can be new, too.

Chapter 5 Review: FRAGMENTS OF LIGHT

LOOK AT YOUR LIFE

The essence of Kintsugi is reconnecting the broken pieces. As you journey through your own story, I invite you to pause and reflect on what "re-connection" truly means in your life. Consider this: true connection often begins with presence, vulnerability, and intention. God's love is the lacquer that provides golden grace to restore us.

PRAY FOR CHANGE

Thank You for meeting me in this place not with shame,
but with compassion. Shape what's shattered into something
new. Shape me, not into who I once was, but into who You
are calling me to become. Fill my cracks with the gold of Your
grace, that I may reflect Your beauty in every scar and seam.
I place my life in Your hands again today. Amen.

ANCHOR YOURSELF

The following verses have anchored me. Feel free to sit
with them for a while or add one that's been speaking to your
heart.

> Heal me, Lord, and I will be healed; save me
> and I will be saved, for you are the one I praise
> (Jeremiah 17:14).

If anything in my story resonates, or if something from
your own comes to mind; there's space below to reflect or
share.

STILLNESS IN MY SEAMS

What might the Creator whisper to His beloved,
seated still and vulnerable; you're safeguarded
and sanded. Don't reach for the mirror just yet;
be still and enjoy the curing part of the process.
—Tynisa Haskins

TRAUMA SCARRED ME BUT triumph strengthened me! The
emotional aroma of being restored in the most delicate and
deliberate way is honeyed—sweet, rich and golden. Every
aspect of my healing was slow and methodical but intentional. My resin didn't dry fast! Redemption often begins in
the stillness; in the moment we choose to stop pouring into
empty vessels and start tending to the sacred ground of our
own soul. In the shadows of our thoughts lie a desire to truly
know ourselves and God.

To know God is to love and trust Him, and that trust creates space for the lasting "inner" change I was seeking. I had
to choose a new way of thinking, grounded in truth rather
than trauma. I started seeing myself not just as a product of
hardship, but as a person capable of growth, change, and joy.
It's astounding how adjusting the way you see something can
shift your mindset and restore your sense of purpose.

Now that you've been sealed, this "abiding" posture is a critical part of your journey.

I encourage you not to rush through this chapter but sit still and allow the Holy Spirit to settle your seams in preparation for the grace, the oil—the gold.

With Kintsugi, although the lacquer must be applied quickly, it takes time to set. The drying process is essential. It takes patience to avoid re-cracking, shrinking or waves. Healing begins in the right environment, one that nurtures both your heart and your faith. Your mindset matters. It shapes how you move from just getting by to living fully. Proverbs 23:7 tells us that as we think, so we become. When you start to see yourself healed, you begin to believe it's possible. And in the stillness, where surrender meets trust, you make room for God to do what only He can.

As you're waiting for the lacquer to set, there's vulnerability before God. He sees you and reveals your true self. He knows us in unexplored places, even the space between our soul and spirit. His divine distinction of DNA down to the different dimensions. Wow! What an intimate awareness.

Sitting in His presence protects our peace. It prepares us to recognize and respond to His whispers. The stillness of this process reforms and binds us to God. The Hebrew word *Qavah* means to bind together with God while waiting with expectation. It's a reminder that hope is active, not passive. While we're waiting for our attitude to change, the atmosphere compels us to worship. We should worship while waiting because it keeps us focused on God and not ourselves. Worship has a way of prioritizing our hearts and reminding us of what matters most. An unknown author once said, "Worship louder in the silence, the louder we lift God's name, the clearer His victory becomes." But maybe the silence isn't just something to fill, maybe it's an invitation. In those still, quiet moments, worship becomes less about sound and more about surrender.

So, how are we communicating that we want to know God in the way He knows us?

We rarely question a surgeon's ability to repair what's broken beneath the surface. We sign the consent form, trust the process, and believe healing is underway, even when we can't see it. But when God, the One who formed us in secret and knows every detail of our design, says He's healed something deep within... we hesitate. We struggle to take Him at His word when He speaks of healing and wholeness.

Isn't that something? The very One who authored life and understands how soul and spirit intertwine offers restoration but we often doubt it, dismiss it, or delay receiving it.

Why is it easier to believe in physical healing than in the quiet, transformative work God does within the heart? I believe our delayed belief—delays our relief. If we receive healing and truly believe it, then our thoughts, words and actions will turn minds and hearts toward heaven.

Have you ever found yourself questioning whether something God gave you was really yours? It's subtle, but the enemy is crafty, planting doubt where there should be confidence. My peace of mind, my purpose, my desires, my voice... all felt negotiable at times, like they could be taken or forfeited. But they weren't given by chance, they were spoken into being by God.

Isaiah 55:11 reminds me of that truth: "So is my word that goes out from my mouth: it will not return to me empty but will accomplish what I desire and achieve the purpose for which I sent it." In other words, if God said it—it's settled. His word doesn't waver, and neither should our trust in what He's already promised.

Carlos Whitaker penned a profound thought, "Beholding is how we begin to notice again, not just what's happening around us but what God is doing within us." We may not be able to physically see the changes God has made on the inside of us but our *re-connection* to the vine will cause our fruit to show and grow. Our spiritual attunement to God allows us to hear and see Him move in ways we might normally miss. I see progress in areas of my life that I once thought were helpless.

Can anybody testify with me what it feels like to be "unbothered" and at peace on the inside, but your spirit hadn't caught up with your face?

Maybe I'm the only one.

For years my facial expressions swung between both sides of the RBF pendulum: 1) Resting Bothered Face and 2) Redeemed But Father...Fix My Face. Lol. I was waiting to be delivered, wishing the Holy Spirit could be my personal ventriloquist. But God didn't remove them at all, He made me more aware so that it didn't hinder my ability to share the gospel. 2 Peter 3:9 says,

The Lord is not slow in keeping his promise, as some understand slowness. Instead, he is patient with you, not wanting anyone to perish, but everyone to come to repentance.

This stillness, this time and season challenged me to completely depend on God. I was healed but not yet whole because more work needed to be done. Work that would bring about a different degree of character and level of maturity in me. Therefore, I chose to be still and to lean into the Holy Spirit.

I know that I was preserved for a purpose!

And it wasn't only to show others what not to do.

I was restored for a mission of love and truth; to speak life into hearts that have lost their way, forgotten their worth, or are mending from life's many shapes and seasons of brokenness.

I didn't readily accept this mission, in fact, the thought of it discouraged me. I wanted to shrink and shut down because of the painful memories that it ignited. Yet, as I sat with those memories, they've become touchpoints to regenerate my desire to help others seal the gaps between the broken pieces of their lives with truth and renewed possibility of transformation.

Of course I have experienced opposition along the way, people and circumstances testing my new nature. The less time I spent in God's presence proved how critical it is to embrace this stillness and shift in my thinking. At this stage in my life, reacting too soon risks reopening old wounds *(re-injury)* or forming new ones. My patient posture became part of protecting my future. It was a protective sealant, not just a one-time event. a renewed way of thinking and living that anchored to solidify my wholeness when my peace was inevitably challenged.

My surrender became less about mending my former self and more about transforming me to look more like Christ. It's in the sacred pause where we stop pouring into what's draining us and start drawing from the well that never runs dry.

Healing isn't just about being put back together; it's about becoming resilient enough to stay whole when life applies pressure in familiar places. This process of healing, like Kintsugi is intentional, slow, and sacred. It requires space and grace. We need that space to breathe, reflect, and grow; and we need the grace to endure setbacks without giving up.

There's often a deep and ongoing wrestle between the inner and outer self. While your spirit is being shaped and refined in the presence of your Creator, you're still walking around in the same physical body carrying old memories, habits, and reflexes. That tension is real. It can feel disorienting when your soul is evolving, but your surroundings and even your own reflection don't seem to reflect that change just yet.

Your human nature, the part of you that clings to what's familiar, can quietly resist the newness God is bringing forth. It tries to slow the work being done on your heart, pulling you back into patterns you're actively trying to outgrow. And some days, it's hard to look in the mirror and believe that anything is different at all.

But the mirror holds more than your image, it offers an invitation. A chance to look beyond the surface and recognize the transformation taking place within. When you pause and truly look inward, you begin to see it: the evidence of spiritual re-creation. It's subtle, but it's there in the softened response, the unexpected peace, the new strength to choose differently. That's the beauty of becoming—it often starts invisibly, but it always grows into something you'll one day recognize clearly.

ASK YOURSELF

Consider these questions not just as prompts, but as gentle mirrors, or ways to examine the depth, the distance, and the desire for introspection:

- Where in your life are you tempted to rush healing or force progress?

- How can you practice patience with yourself and with God in this season of becoming?

- What small signs of growth might you be overlooking because they don't look like a finished product yet?

We all struggle with patience. However, some things require patience to smooth out the rough edges. Patience is about the process of refinement. God uses the stillness to attune our hearts and renew our minds. While we wait, we should temper our expectations to one that values the purity of God's process. We shouldn't want to experience healing but not fully embrace wholeness because of our old mentality. We don't want to mishandle God's deliverance by neglecting spiritual disciplines. By actively nurturing my spiritual well-being and tending to my own heart; my refortified frame is now strong enough for a life of purpose and service to others.

Restoring our sense of purpose happens in God's presence. We live to serve God through serving each other. Yet, it's difficult to give what we don't have, and the oxygen mask analogy becomes very real. Instead of securing my own mask first through prayer and meditation, I prioritized everything else; energy, attention, and emotional reserves, pouring it all into metaphorical leaky tanks, hoping it will somehow hold me together. Placing the oxygen mask on myself isn't selfish, it's obedience. It was and is an act of trust in who was transforming me. I needed a holy yielding of what I could not fix, releasing it all to the One who could handle it all. Healing doesn't happen through control; it happens through surrender! Let the Holy Spirit seal and fill us so that we can pour into others...God's love and light.

Once you commit to being restored, give yourself some grace and *be patient with the process*. Watching paint dry may not be fun, but waiting ensures the paint remains intact. Depending on what you're painting *(what's being restored)*, stepping back to admire the art from different angles and at various stages can give clarity regarding direction for the next stroke *(step)*. It also enables you to see the canvas *(your life)* in a unique way.

The best thing about transformation is knowing that change is coming and feeling the change occurring. Yes, it takes time, but it begins with intention. So, take advantage of any time you get to abide in God's presence and behold what He is doing. Allow the adhesives of hope, love, and acceptance to seal the broken pieces of your heart together. Your heart may not look like it once did, but it now tells a story of survival, surrender, and sacred rebuilding. It becomes living evidence that healing is possible, and the presence of cracks doesn't mean the absence of value.

Chapter 6 Review: FRAGMENTS OF LIGHT

LOOK AT YOUR LIFE

Transformation takes time and that can be frustrating when you just want to feel better, be better, or move on already. But real change, the kind that reshapes your heart and renews your mind, often happens slowly, quietly, and beneath the surface. It's okay if you're not "there" yet. What matters is that you're willing to stay in the process, to trust God with the in-between, and to be gentle with yourself along the way. It's important to receive that transformation with grace and allow yourself to grow into it. When you walk in that grace, it not only honors the healing you've done, it also strengthens how you'll face challenges moving forward, with clarity, confidence, and peace.

PRAY FOR CHANGE

Lord, I confess, I often want quick results and instant healing. I get discouraged when I don't see the progress I hoped for or when I feel stuck in the same struggles. But I know You're not rushed by time the way I am. You're steady, intentional, and always working even when I can't see it.

Help me to trust the slow work You're doing in me. Give me the grace to be patient with the process, to be kind to myself while I grow, and to believe that every small step matters. Remind me that transformation is not about perfection but about presence, Yours and mine, together. You are making something beautiful in me. Amen.

ANCHOR YOURSELF

The following verses have anchored me. Feel free to sit with it for a while or add one that's been speaking to your heart.

> Abide in Me, and I in you. As the branch cannot bear fruit of itself unless it abides in the vine, so neither can you unless you abide in Me (John 15:4).

If anything in my story resonates, or if something from your own comes to mind; there's space below to reflect or share.

Chapter Seven

<u>Veins of Light</u>

Every crack, every layer is valued. Beautiful. Whole. Now the world will see what I always saw in you. Do you see what I see? It may not be what you were expecting. But I hope you are pleasantly surprised. –Tynisa Haskins

My gold lines aren't just shining, they're testifying. Not only have I been restored, I have been redefined. Each crack is a glowing memory rather than a blemish. My repaired heart is beginning to show strength through vulnerability. My cracks are no longer something to hide; they are evidence of grace at work in my life by the gold running through the pain.

I am no longer who I once was. In God's hands, I've been made new, marked not by what broke me, but by the beauty of what now holds me together. In the midst of life's busyness and constant demands, I stand, flawed yet grounded in growth. The woman I aspire to be isn't disconnected from who I was. In fact, she is emerging from every version of me I've ever been. My character is being refined, my heart steadily healed. I am evolving with intention.

With my heart silent and surrendered. I was ready for the "gold powder" to be applied to my cracks. Yes, the gold glitters but it only looks good if the groundwork has been done right. God's handiwork inside of me is a key part of the beauty appreciated outside of me. As I seek a deeper level of fulfillment, I wonder—did I create enough space for Holy Spirit to fill me with oil so that my lamp can burn bright for as long as it's required?

Have you facilitated a workspace for God?

Try not to focus on "what" you went through but "why" you went through it. I believe God wants to use your experience to educate, elevate and encourage you. Don't let the restored version of you become an ashtray of agitation, collecting the smoldering remnants of pain and unspoken apologies. The cracks may remain, but they shine. They do not shine because you were made whole by the person who broke you, but because you chose to heal anyway. Closure isn't a gift someone else delivers. It's the gold you pour into your own fractures, even when the "sorry" never comes.

Some people are so traumatized by what happened to them, they cannot see what's right in front of them, hope and healing. Letting go may feel risky, but it could be the very thing that invites deeper connection, richer grace, and unexpected strength.

Don't wait for their apology to begin your healing. Only God can truly restore what was broken. Your path forward begins with obedience to Matthew 5:44: love your enemies and pray for those who have hurt you. I used to focus my attention solely on my "enemies" versus my "inner me." My healing began the moment I stopped rehearsing the pain and started accepting what happened, not as defeat, but as a chapter God is redeeming.

The road I took became a trail for my deliverance.

I used to carry shame and embarrassment over my parents' addiction, as if a silent banner trailed behind me, exposing the dysfunction I tried so hard to hide. I used to think my identity was defined by my family and my deepest sorrow. I feared being defined by my pain.

What you think you see isn't always what you get, especially when imperfections are visible. Assumptions about my age, background, or intelligence led to some awkward encounters, yet those same conversations often uncovered my maturity, identity, and character. Those imperfections, once sources of shame, became catalysts for growth. And now, they don't just show where I've been, they help me shine. It is in that light, His light, that I return to the mirror once more, not to critique, but to truly see.

Oh dear mirror, my eyes now see
The beauty hidden inside of me.
Look who I've become, refined through grace
No longer lost in that broken place.

My sealed cracks now boldly shine,
Each piece aligned by a hand divine.
No trace remains of where I cracked
Now a masterpiece, mended and fully intact.

This new reflection staring back at me
Is a one-of-a-kind mark of God's artistry.
Pinch me, please! This can't be real,
But freedom has come, no more masks to conceal.

Thank you, mirror, for showing what's true
The path was hard, but it carried me through.
Each journey unfolds in its time,
But healing comes, line by line.

Now I know what wholeness truly means,
Not the absence of wounds but the peace between.

If trials return, I'll stand and see
Each scar reflects His victory in me.

Who you choose to be matters! I choose to be a healed and restored version of myself.

Throughout my life, people would often say I looked like my mother. For a long time, that resemblance unsettled me because—to me, it meant I might become like her and I couldn't imagine anything more frightening. But with time, I've come to see that looking like someone doesn't mean inheriting their choices. It simply means carrying a part of their story, which I do, and it is a part I'm still learning how to hold with grace.

Who you are at your core, shapes how you live, how you love, and how you lead?

Let go of who you were known to be. Your transformation has opened a new window, and it is a sacred invitation for lasting change.

Step through it. "Redefine what your wholeness looks like and make something beautiful out of the life you have" (Altman, A., n.d.). The window of my soul is no longer filled with shattered pieces. The worst of me became the best of me as life experiences led me to my destiny.

One experience in particular stands out: I grew up in a time when children were expected to be seen, not heard. Silence was a form of obedience, and I learned early on that "a hard head made a soft bottom." So, I kept my thoughts to myself. While I found my voice at school and through poetry; outside those spaces, I rarely spoke, reserving my words for only those closest to me. Ironically, today, my husband and children often tell me I talk too loudly and too much. It makes me smile because it's just like God to take the very parts of us we once silenced or devalued and use them in powerful ways.

There is strength in reclaiming your voice, even if it trembled in silence for years. There is beauty in restoration, in allowing God to take the fragments of your story and craft something resilient, radiant, and new. I no longer shy away from my volume literal or figurative. My voice is part of my redemption, a reminder that what was once stifled can be set free, and what was once broken can become the very thing that inspires others to heal too.

Shaped by a past that tried to define me; mixed with the challenge of figuring out how to move forward, I believe my best is yet to come. I decided to prioritize rest and restoration. Now is the perfect time to seek wholeness intentionally and daily. Healing isn't passive. It's a choice, a commitment to show up for myself the way I've shown up for everyone else.

True freedom begins with a shift in how you see yourself, God, others, and the choices you make. I am fearfully and wonderfully made; uniquely fashioned by my Creator. I walk confidently in peace as I relentlessly pursue God's purpose for my life. I may be invisible to some, but His light is undeniable, and it shines through me.

Transformation is not just behavior change; it's the outward evidence that your inner reality has been reshaped by grace. Each small act of love and moment of peace is sacred, too.

And so, I say this gently to myself: You've made beautiful progress. Don't rush past it. Don't minimize it. Recognize it and Celebrate it.

The Kintsugi process is a beautiful reflection of restoration; it doesn't deny the cracks; it honors them. It isn't about becoming someone new, it's about finally embracing who you've always been, beneath the brokenness. Isaiah 61:3 reminds us that God gives "a crown of beauty instead of ashes, the oil of joy instead of mourning."

The damaged pottery is not concealed; rather, it is carefully restored and repurposed. This process reflects the heart of God as He acknowledges human suffering, engages with it, and offers healing that creates a sense of purpose. As Arielle Altman said, "Cracks represent your story. The gold is [your crowning] glory and a celebration. It's not about a cover-up but a highlight of your journey."

Now, I hope people see my cracks and recognize the light emanating from the gold that sealed them; I want them to understand the reasons behind my radiance. So, don't look back with shame at what you've healed from or overcome. Look around with awe. Admire the strength it took to get here. Let those golden lines speak boldly of your resilience, your growth, and God's grace.

My golden lines have a lot to say, so what narrative do I want to carry forward?

I decided to break the cycle of generational trauma; I courageously chose to disrupt the legacy of believing Satan's lies and acting on them. This is my spiritual act of defiance: saying "no" to the narrative that had long bound me, and "yes" to a new story rooted in truth, with the courage to begin again. Breaking the cycle wasn't just about walking away from what hurt me, it was about walking toward who I was always meant to be. And maybe that's the question for all of us:

ASK YOURSELF

- What cycle are you being invited to break, and what kind of beauty might rise in its place?

- Have you embraced the new version of who you're becoming?

- In what ways can you begin to align your next steps

with what truly matters: values, principles, or truths that reflect who you're becoming in Christ? *(Think about what's guiding your choices right now. Are they rooted in fear or faith, bitterness or forgiveness? What shifts could help realign your path with God's heart for you?)*

"Arise, shine, for your light has come, and the glory of the Lord rises upon you" (Isaiah 60:1) is more than a call to awaken. It's an offer to step into wholeness. This rising is not just about standing; it's about shining from within. The light shines because God filled those wounds with purpose, and beauty. In Him, we are not just repaired; we are redeemed.

God's expression of love through me looks different from anyone else because He prepared me for such a time as this. My healing wasn't exclusively for me. It's about me sharing how God showed up in my story, rescued me so that I can help others find Him too. This "glow up" isn't about how I feel, it's about acting on what I believe and know is true. Faith is forward motion with a filled heart and freed mind. God is not asking me to do something impossible; He's asking me to do a hard thing with a healed heart to help others find freedom through His light that shines within me.

Restoration is a gift to all of us. We have much to give even when we feel empty. Some of us have untapped potential waiting to be realized and illuminated. Restoration reveals your beauty in brokenness and lets you share your story to help others become whole.

Chapter 7 Review: FRAGMENTS OF LIGHT

LOOK AT YOUR LIFE

If you ever wondered if anything good can come from your pain; the answer is "Yes," and that good may be as good as gold! There's a beauty that only comes after the breaking. A strength that's only visible when the pieces are regathered. Kintsugi isn't just an art, it's a metaphor for what God does with us.

After being mended, shaped, and held together by God's grace; I see the beauty in every broken place. I'm not who I was, and that's a good thing. This healing hasn't just made me whole; it's helped me rediscover my worth and value in the hands of the One who lovingly put me back together with purpose in every piece.

PRAY FOR CHANGE

Lord, thank You for seeing beyond my brokenness and loving me through every step of becoming. I surrender the old versions of myself, the one shaped by fear, doubt, and shame. I welcome the new me You are refining with grace. The cracks once made me feel worthless, but now I see how You've filled them with purpose. Where I saw damage, You saw design. Where I felt shame, You poured grace. Help me to walk boldly in the identity You've given me. I'm beginning to see myself the way You always have: precious, whole, and worthy of love.

Help me to walk forward, not hiding my story, but honoring it. Let the gold in my scars reflect Your goodness. May I never forget that my value was never lost, it was being rediscovered all along. Amen.

ANCHOR YOURSELF

The following verse has anchored me. Feel free to sit with it for a while or add one that's been speaking to your heart.

Your word is a lamp for my feet, a light on my path. (Psalm 119:105)

If anything in my story resonates, or if something from your own comes to mind; there's space below to refflect or share.

_____

_____

_____

_____

_____

_____

_____

_____

_____

_____

_____

_____

_____

_____

_____

_____

_____

_____

_____

_____

_____

_____

_____

MY
BREAKTHROUGH

You were shaped with purpose, touched by grace. Now go, reflect the hands that formed you. Don't be shy, lift the veil, let them see. Behold your beauty. Be brave. Be bold. –Tynisa Haskins

BROKENNESS DOESN'T DISQUALIFY US—IT prepares us for our designated assignments. Now that healing has come, I find myself wondering, what comes next? What do I do with this restored version of me, the one no longer held together by sheer effort, but gently sustained by grace?

Sometimes, healing begins not in fixing what's broken, but in allowing others to see the cracks. We don't have to look like what we've been through; we can rise above those struggles and look even better despite them. I really believe we all have something meaningful to offer this world. Not in spite of our flaws, but sometimes because of them. Each of us carries a one-of-a-kind story, a gift shaped by both joy and struggle. And more often than not, it's the cracks in our lives that let the light break through, reminding us and others that beauty can still be found in broken places.

So what about you?

Have you taken a moment to consider the beauty you carry even in the places you once tried to hide? You, too, are a one-of-a-kind gift. Maybe it's time to stop disqualifying yourself and start seeing the light that's been shining through you all along.

Today, as I look back on the journey that brought me to true joy, I'm deeply grateful. I didn't come this far to let life's hardships define me or derail my destiny; I chose to be better, not bitter.

I used to look in the mirror and see a mask barely covering a mess, but now I see a warrior. Am I scarred? Yes, but those scars are traced in gold. The bitterness of my trials has been transformed into the beauty of triumph.

Those who knew me before, only encountered a fragment of who I was. They saw a version shaped by survival, not identity. I resist the urge to doubt the authenticity of my transformation. This is not a performance. This is presence. I don't need to "fake it till I make it" because there's nothing fake about the beauty God has uncovered in me. The gold in my cracks doesn't need to be hidden, they are proof that I've been healed and that I'm healing still. The hardest part now is learning to accept my new self, not as a stranger, but as someone I've been becoming all along.

Too often, we stay trapped in our trauma, replaying the damage, unable to accept grace or extend forgiveness. But imagine Jesus, seeing you broken, angry, and lost; choosing you anyway, calling you His, and reminding you who you are in Him. That's grace. That's love. Transformation reveals that what you've learned has finally settled into your soul. Even after healing begins to take root, it can be hard to recognize the wholeness within you or to believe that you're truly free, no longer bound by who you used to be. But unless you walk in the freedom God gave you, you'll keep reliving the very bondage He already delivered you from. And that freedom, is foundational to your frame. It gives you the strength to stand tall, even when others try to shrink you with their expectations.

Both Jonathan Evans (Tony Evan's Podcast, 2025, 17:50) and his father, Dr. Tony Evans, speak powerfully about releasing the past in order to embrace the future. Jonathan poses a challenging question, and I'd like you to consider it: is it even possible to rid yourself of trauma? Jonathan Evans suggests that some people become so familiar with hurt that they make a home in it. Even when they've been brought out, the pain never truly leaves them because they haven't let it go. They remain so bitter about the past that they never become seasoned for the promise ahead. In this context, salt doesn't preserve, it stagnates. There's no growth, no life, only a cycle of disappointment and delay.

But Galatians 5:1 offers a different path: "For freedom Christ has set us free; stand firm therefore, and do not submit again to a yoke of slavery."

It reminds us that while we've been set free, it's still possible to return to the bondage we've known. The question is, *why would we?* Especially after tasting what it means to be made new. As Dr. Tony Evans so wisely stated, "God can take the good, the bad, and the ugly and create a masterpiece called your destiny." That truth became real for me. I no longer live shackled to the pain of my past. Instead, I walk forward; restored, redeemed, and marked by grace. The gold in my cracks is no accident; it's evidence of divine craftsmanship.

You can have this wholeness and freedom, too.

What does breakthrough look like? It depends.

I found it easier to first identify myself apart from the negative experience. I am Tynisa, period.

My exposure to alcoholism and drug addiction doesn't overshadow the other hard things I've walked through, like serving in a combat zone or working in toxic environments. Each of those experiences left cracks. And while they shaped me, they didn't determine the end of my story.

Breaking through may feel daunting, but until you take that first step, you'll never know just how far you can go. Faith doesn't guarantee ease or immediate results, it invites us to keep showing up, even when the outcome is uncertain. I didn't need twelve steps to move toward healing—just one leap of faith.

Healing demands honesty.

It isn't going to make you feel comfortable, but it will make you divinely better.

Ironically, this book is all about healing my broken heart, but the process itself required something even more uncomfortable: owning the breakage within me (acknowledging the cracks in my soul). One honest, intentional decision to say: I'm broken, even in places I can't see... and I don't want to stay this way. Brokenness doesn't always look like visible wounds. That's the hard part, when the pain isn't seen, it's easier to ignore.

We rush to the ER when we're bleeding but hesitate to bring our wounds to God. Maybe because they're hidden, or maybe because it feels safer to stay numb. It takes courage to trust and lay every shattered piece in the hands that formed you, to put you back together. I used to think healing meant getting stronger or pulling myself together. But over time, I've come to realize that true healing started when I stopped pretending and came to God with a heart that was humbled, and willing to be reshaped.

Psalm 51:17 says that God doesn't despise a broken spirit or a contrite heart. That verse has stayed with me, especially in the moments when I felt like I had nothing left to offer. It reminds me that God isn't looking for perfection, He's looking for surrender. And in that surrender, wholeness begins. That truth has shaped the way I view healing; a journey marked by honest attempts, setbacks, and grace along the way.

Walking alongside someone battling addiction can be a heart-wrenching rhythm of "highs" that swing wildly, fueled by substances or self-destructive patterns. Every high—a heartbeat closer to silence. Every binge—a step deeper into the fog. And all the while, the world keeps spinning as if nothing's wrong. Yet we're holding on for dear life, doing our best to stay grounded and shield the ones we love from the ripple effects of the chaos that threatens to consume everything in its path.

My mother attempted the 12-step program more than once, and though it never brought the results we'd prayed for, I believe she'd be proud to know that my path to healing didn't require twelve steps. For me, it took one serious act of surrender. That didn't erase the pain, but it did plant hope. It was the moment I chose to believe that healing was possible, even if I didn't know exactly how it would unfold, it was my declaration. I refused to stay stuck in the story of what hurt me. I choose the possibility of something better.

I think of my mother often, especially when I reflect on my journey. Her struggle taught me compassion, her efforts (even when they didn't lead to lasting change) taught me perseverance. And though she didn't experience the breakthrough she fought for, her attempts left footprints for me to follow, even if my path veered in a different direction.

It took me a while, but I stand confident in my purpose, even now when others try to define my actions or question my path. Their opinions don't dictate my obedience. God does! I enjoy the warmth of my current condition like a mug of meaningful memories that can be filled up and carried with me. I stand in the tension between what was, what is, and what's still becoming; choosing, each day, to move forward in wholeness, even when the process feels slow. When confronted with the enemy's schemes, we have to respond differently with wisdom instead of reaction, faith instead of fear. Each deliberate choice becomes an act of alignment, drawing us closer to the fullness of who God always intended for us to be.

ASK YOURSELF

This reflection is not about having the right answers. It's about listening more closely to your heart, to grace, and to the God who has been with you all along.

- What does "moving forward" look like; are you ready to take a step forward?

- Where have you experienced unexpected healing or strength?

- What truth will you carry with you from this chapter into this season of your life?

Healing looks different for all of us.

Because growth isn't a straight line; it's a winding path, full of starts and stops. Life will keep showing up with new challenges, and each time, you rise a little differently and stronger, wiser, more self-aware. The gold in my story hasn't been poured in all at once, it's been applied slowly, choice by choice. The decision to forgive. The bravery to speak. The wisdom to rest. The risk to love. The desire to grow. Every intentional act sealed another crack with purpose.

For some, it's a series of structured steps. For others, it's a messy, winding road paved by faith and tiny acts of courage. Bravely pursuing breakthrough isn't easy, it requires effort.

Wanting change is one thing, desire alone doesn't carry you through the hard work of healing. It takes courage to face what's been broken, patience to sit with the pain, and faith to believe something beautiful can come from it. That's why Kintsugi speaks so deeply to me.

It doesn't just patch up the cracks—it elevates them. It illuminates the purpose of the pain and reminds me that healing isn't about erasing the past but honoring the journey that brought me here.

I honor my mother's journey even as I walk my own, and I carry her with me as a quiet strength, woven into the gold of my restoration. My healing is my legacy. And building it begins now. I hope my resilience and encouragement are etched into the hearts, minds, and stories of those who knew me then and those who are getting to know me now.

While you only got a glimpse of who I am through these pages, I hope you felt inspired to lean into the present and take a leap that leads you toward living more wholly, purposefully, and freely.

So, if you're standing on the edge of a decision, unsure whether healing is possible, just know, it doesn't begin with perfection. It begins with permission. God doesn't need you to have it all together; He just wants your "yes."

Bring your baggage. Bring your anger, your aches, your unanswered questions. Bring them all, from the shadows to the surface. Then take your own bold step toward restoration. Your broken pieces are not the end of your story; they're the beginning of your masterpiece.

You've been made new. Now it's time to walk in your purpose.

And how do you share that purpose with the world?

That's the work of art only you can create.

Now that your season of "heart work" is finished, a harvest of hope and gratitude awaits you.

Chapter 8 Review: FRAGMENTS OF LIGHT

LOOK AT YOUR LIFE

We made it! I hope it was an interesting and introspective ride.

At the close of every story that moves us, we're often left with more questions than answers, and that's a good thing. You've walked through pages filled with pain, beauty, resilience, and redemption. This final chapter isn't an ending, it's a threshold. A moment to breathe, to gather what's been uncovered, and to ask yourself what comes next. Before you move forward, take time to sit with all that has surfaced. Let this space be one of quiet honesty. You are not who you were when you started, and that matters.

PRAY FOR CHANGE

God, thank You for being present in every part of my story, especially the broken chapters. I want to move beyond this hurt into my breakthrough. Help me to find courage in my vulnerability as I trust You enough to take the next step forward. Open my heart to receive your peace as you piece me back together. May my healing invite others into their own, and may my story become a vessel for hope. Amen.

ANCHOR YOURSELF

The following verse has anchored me. Feel free to sit with it for a while or add one that's been speaking to your heart.

> To bestow on them a crown of beauty instead of ashes, the oil of joy instead of mourning, and a garment of praise instead of a spirit of despair. They will be called oaks of righteousness,

a planting of the Lord for the display of his splen-
dor (Isaiah 61:3).

If anything in my story resonates, or if something from
your own comes to mind; there's space below to reflect or
share.

REFERENCES

WORKS CITED

Altman, A. [@dr.alexa_altman]. (2019, February 7). Posts [Alexa Altman, PHD]. Instagram. Retrieved August 4, 2024, from

Tennant, Ella - Lecturer. (2024, January 29). How the philosophy behind the Japanese art form of "kintsugi" can help us navigate failure. The Conversation.

Evans, T. (2017). Tony Evans Study Bible. Holman Bible Publishers.

Evans, T. (Tony Evan's Podcast). (2025, April 21). Podcast episode "Past or Promise" [Audio podcast]. Retrieved from

Evans, T. (2011). Victory In Spiritual Warfare (1st ed., p. 72). Harvest House Publishers.

Holy Bible, New International Version®, NIV® Copyright ©1973, 1978, 1984, 2011 by Biblica, Inc.® Used by permission. All rights reserved worldwide

Whittaker, C. (n.d.). *The spiritual discipline of beholding.* Proverbs 31 Ministries | Devotions {Encouragement for Today}. https://proverbs31.org/read/devotions/full-post/2025/07/07/the-spiritual-discipline-of-beholding

WORKS REFERENCED

Jurevicius, O., & Bastien, D. (2024, March 21). The Johari window model: All you need to know - SM insight. Strategic Management Insight.

Mate, Dr Gabor. 2018. In the Realm of Hungry Ghosts. London, England: Vermilion.

ABOUT THE AUTHOR

Tynisa is a retired Air Force veteran with over 26 years of leadership and service. Following military retirement, she worked in workforce development, helping individuals and communities build skills, find direction, and pursue meaningful careers.

Now an entrepreneur, Tynisa dedicates her work to speaking, writing, consulting, facilitating, and coaching—guiding others toward purpose-driven leadership, personal growth, and resilient transformation. She holds a Master's degree in Education from Liberty University and brings both strategic insight and a deep passion for empowering others into every endeavor.

When not writing or working with clients, Tynisa enjoys swimming, crafting, and spending quality time with friends and family.

instagram.com/scripted.messages
linkedin.com/in/tynisa-haskins

www.ingramcontent.com/pod-product-compliance
Lightning Source LLC
Chambersburg PA
CBHW070349130626
46556CB00007B/3099